What Am I Waiting For?

What Am I Waiting For?

I Need a Life Coach Now!

Terry Hite

iUniverse, Inc.
Bloomington

What Am I Waiting For?
I Need a Life Coach Now!

iUniverse books may be ordered through booksellers or by contacting:

iUniverse
1663 Liberty Drive
Bloomington, IN 47403
www.iuniverse.com
1-800-Authors (1-800-288-4677)

ISBN: 978-1-4759-8602-0 (sc)
ISBN: 978-1-4759-8604-4 (hc)
ISBN: 978-1-4759-8603-7 (ebk)

Library of Congress Control Number: 2013907425

Printed in the United States of America

iUniverse rev. date: 04/26/2013

Contents

Preface

I've struggled with writing this preface, trying to find the right words. I've changed the text, erased it completely, put back some parts of it, changed it again, and then decided to just *do it* and pray for the best!

A wise king once said, "What has been will be again, what has been done will be done again; there is nothing new under the sun" (Ecclesiastes 1:9, NIV). I have found that to be true and so would like to reveal a story about life's experiences that was first told ages ago and has been repeated over and over again. In order to not repeat the story again, mines are from a perspective of my living during a period of time that's kindly communicating different ideas and ways of living life.

Over the years, I have searched for a reason for why we do the things that we do. I have read many motivational, spiritual, and self-help books to try to make some sense of our existence. My experience for writing this book comes from one of life's greatest teachers—*living life on its own terms*. I was born in Virginia and grew up in New York State. I later moved to Washington, DC, and, having gotten tired of the traffic, now reside in North Carolina. Looking back over the years, I noticed that my spiritual journey had taken the same path and led me down the road to draw the same conclusions about life. The old saying "God is good" is just as true today as it was yesterday.

Anyone can coach you in life—your mom or dad, your minister or school teacher, your friend or coworker. Any of those people can offer guidance on living life, and they can all give you perfectly good advice. But can they give you what you really need to live your life with purpose? That is why I wrote this book. Maybe you don't have anyone to talk to regarding your life situations; maybe you want someone to offer you constructive criticism or objective feedback; or maybe you want help from someone who won't take advantage of you. Ultimately, I want you to think about making a shift in your consciousness that will allow you to move to the next level of your life. If you are feeling trapped you don't have to stay trapped because there is an answer to getting control over your life.

Acknowledgments

First, I would like to thank my heavenly Father, God, who helped me in completing this book successfully.

Second, I would like to thank my parents, particularly my mother, Pearl. My parents are no longer with us, but they have equally inspired me to write this book.

Third, I would like to thank my siblings, nieces, nephews, and a host of other relatives who, throughout most of my life, showed me how to live with purpose.

Last but not least, I am very thankful to an army of friends, both old and new, who have supported me, for it is mostly out of a deep appreciation to them that I have completed my book effectively. Moreover, I would like to give a special thanks to William and to offer this book in remembrance of my beloved friend Hattie.

Introduction

We are all seeking our higher self in some capacity. Whether we want mental stability, emotional wellness, spiritual healing, physical health, or deeper, more meaningful relationships, each of us is striving for that next level of beingness that will allow us to discard the rags of mediocrity and leave them behind us.

The unnamed force that drives this striving compels us to reach higher, run faster, endure longer, and stand stronger—not because we *want* to but because we *have* to. We feel as if there aren't any other options, so we press forward because to remain stagnant means that we're somehow dying a slow, agonizing, and mind-numbing death.

At some point in our lives, we had a vision of what our ideal life would look like. We were aspiring to be successful in our career, in our family life, and in our social circle. Many of us had visions of where we wanted to live, how many children we wanted to raise, the type of impact we wanted to make on the world, and how we would influence those closest to us.

But somewhere along the way something changed. We became more jaded, more skeptical, and less optimistic about those dreams coming true. Our visions plummeted on the scale and went from ten down to five, and in many cases we can't even explain how and when it happened.

But the good news is that there are people out there who care about whether you reach your goals. These people help you get focused and stay focused. They rally around you in your time of need and show you why energy goes where your focus flows. There are people who champion your cause because it's what they love to do. These people are life coaches.

The Age of the New Normal

So what is or what was "normal"? If we were back in the 1950s, normal would likely be a one-income household. The father's role would be to go to work regularly, loyally, and faithfully for thirty or forty years and then retire with a gold watch and some form of recognition. The mother's role would be to stay at home and manage the household, which included tasks like doing the laundry, cleaning the house, running errands, cooking, and taking care of the children. When the children came home from school, their mother would be there. She would help them with their homework and when their father came home from work they would eat dinner. They would have family time and then it was off to bed.

On the weekend both parents would likely spend time with their children, attending their baseball games, dance recitals, and stage plays as well as bake sales, state fairs, and local farmers markets. Families would also take regular vacations together, allowing their children to form meaningful memories and learn about the world beyond their own neighborhood.

Yes, in the 1950s and even the '60s this all would have been considered "normal," but what's normal in our society has undergone several facelifts. In fact, what's normal in the new millennium isn't even close to what was a normal fifty or sixty year ago. The structure of the typical American household from back then is basically obsolete today. The vast majority of today's households function on a two-person income, and the children themselves get jobs once they become of working age.

Beyond the household, even the structure of the family itself has changed. A family is no longer just a man and a woman and their children. A family can comprise a single parent and his or her children, a cohabitating heterosexual couple, a same-sex couple and their children, and so on.

The once-standard nine-to-five, forty-hour workweek is gone. For many if not most people it has been replaced by a fifty-to-sixty-hour workweek, and with advances in technology, workers are reachable around the clock. The feeling of having job security has dissipated, and the fear or reality of losing one's job has spawned an entrepreneurial revolution. According to the US Department of Labor and Bureau of Labor Statistics, since the early 90's many working Americans have started their own business of some kind. This entrepreneurial trend has been recognized by colleges and universities across the country, with more courses focusing on entrepreneurship being offered than ever before. And rightfully so, as more and more people are starting to understand that, in order to be secure, you have to create security yourself—no more looking to corporations to provide for your future.

I recall coaching one of my clients who was an entrepreneur and worked from home. She told me that things had gotten so overwhelming work-wise that she decided to hire interns. Initially she met resistance from colleges and universities because they were concerned about students being in a stranger's home. That concern is completely understandable, of course, but eventually, she said, the schools became more flexible. They began to see that as entrepreneurship was growing, so were entrepreneurs' needs for interns. As a result they incorporated home-based internships into their program.

But even our idea of colleges and universities themselves has changed drastically over the decades. While we still have the option of attending a brick-and-mortar institution, we are now able to earn credits and degrees from home, at our computer. Thirty years ago such an option would have been unheard of, but today it is quite common.

The way we conduct research while in school, or the way we get information for work or for our own projects, is different today than the way it was just twenty years ago. Back then you would walk into a library, smile at the librarians, thumb through the card catalog, and make your way over to a section of books and locate the material you needed. You were mindful not to make too much noise because there were many other people in the library studying or working. Both the smell of dusty books and the sound of pages turning were prevalent. If at any point you got lost and didn't know where to turn, there was always someone sitting at a desk ready to assist you. Once you found the information you were seeking, you would then check out your books and leave the library mindful of the date you had to return them. While going to the library is still something many people do, it's much more convenient to conduct your research from your computer via search engines on the Internet. Today, the word *Google* is a verb!

And speaking of the Internet, I once had a client who worked in retail for many years. He said that around the mid-nineties his company had started to notice a decline in sales. "The decline started out very slowly," he said, "but as the years progressed our numbers declined more and more. We started to notice a trend among our retail outlets. The numbers simply weren't what we wanted them to be, and we wasted a lot of money beefing up our marketing campaigns." He then said something that really resonated with me. "We started to notice an increase in our online sales simultaneous to a decrease in our retail stores. Then we realized that we were refocusing our marketing dollars in the wrong place," he added. "We restructured our marketing campaigns so that we were focusing more on online sales, and that's when we found the sweet spot." See, people still enjoy walking into stores so that they can touch the clothes, smell the perfume, test the makeup, and try on the accessories. But there are some people who would rather make their purchases with a simple click of a mouse. The bottom line is that people like to have options.

So what is normal? The new normal is that there is no "normal." The term and concept has evolved in step with an increasingly complex and demanding society. If you're a single person who lives alone, considers your best friends to be your family, and eats dinner when you get home from work at nine o'clock, then that is the new normal for you. If you're a business owner who makes business transactions from home all day long while never changing out of your pajamas, then that is the definition of normal for you.

Normal behavior refers to a lack of significant deviation from the average. So if someone is deemed not normal, it simply means that his or her behavior is not common when compared to the majority. What's notable is that those of us who choose the old-school way of doing things are now considered not normal.

A household with a married couple and children where the husband goes to work regularly and the wife stays home and tends to the household is, according to today's society, not normal.

Working forty hours a week for thirty to forty years at the same company and then retiring is not normal.

Getting a college degree without using some form of technology is not normal.

Conducting your research by primarily going to the library, checking out books, and talking to a librarian is not normal.

Doing one-hundred percent of your shopping in a store is not normal.

So what does all this talk about what's "normal" have to do with getting a life coach? The term *Life coach* wasn't even around in the '50s, but in today's world selecting a life coach to help meet your goals is becoming very practical and is a tremendous help when trying to keep up with—and even define—the new normal being created every day.

Undoubtedly, there has certainly been a shift in consciousness and there has been a dynamic paradigm shift with regard to the way we live our lives, make our decisions, and navigate our challenges.

Working with a Life Coach

When pursuing any goal, it's important that you surround yourself with the right people. What do I mean by the "right" people? I mean people who have a genuine desire to see you succeed. The right people are those who will stand with you against the obstacles of the world. They will have your best interest at heart, and they will operate in an ethical manner to elevate you. Simply stated, their goal is to help you achieve *your* goal.

I'm sure you're pretty smart on your own and that you've earned all the accolades, awards, and success you've enjoyed so far. But the smartest move you can make is to surround yourself with people who know things you don't. This idea is at the root of the teacher/student relationship. What sense does it make to have a classroom full of students but no teacher? With no one to educate those less knowledgeable, the result is a group of people trying to figure out something they have no experience with. Talk about the blind leading the blind! A circle made up of people who all have the same level of knowledge and the same measures of strengths is a stagnant circle. Nobody grows, nobody gets ahead, and nobody evolves.

A mentor of mine once said, "If I want to know your present situation, I will look at your friends. If I want to know your future, I will look at your coaches." What he meant by that is simple: the direction of your future can be determined by the direction of those you choose to follow, and the ideal person to show you exactly where you're headed is a life coach.

Even though there are some who consider me to be a successful entrepreneur, I have worked hard all of my life to become an example to people around me, and I suppose in many ways I am. Climbing the ladder of what some may consider success alone is absolutely unheard of. My standing firmly against so many of life's obstacles can easily be attributed to coaches I've had who have helped me lay a strong foundation upon which my goals could stand. They steered me in the right direction so I could take that next step, even if I was terrified to do so. They helped me to hit the ground running.

> It is probably not love that makes the world go around, but rather those mutually supportive alliances through which partners recognize their dependence on each other for the achievement of shared and private goals.
>
> —Fred A. Allen

Building a Strong Alliance

To help you understand some of the benefits of working with a life coach, I have broken them down in a manner that is easily understandable:

Communication: A life coach helps you to better articulate your thoughts in a succinct and clear manner. He or she is in a position to help you clearly define your desired outcome(s).

Organization: A life coach helps you construct a clear strategic plan for reaching your goals.

Accountability: A life coach ensures that you are properly executing your strategic plan.

Connections: A life coach offers you resources that you may not have access to otherwise.

Habits: A life coach helps you develop new habits that will allow you to maximize your desired results.

When most people hear the word *coach,* they think of world-class athletes. Every serious athlete has a coach who serves as an outside observer of his or her actions. If the athlete isn't following through when he's shooting the basketball, or if she isn't consistently hitting the ball on her tennis swing, the coach, as an observer with a certain level of expertise, identifies the shortcoming and works with the athlete to correct it.

It's important to understand that coaches don't need to have performed at the same level the athlete has. What they need is a certain kind of proficiency. Phil Jackson, coach of the Chicago Bulls from 1989 to 1998, was no Michael Jordan, but he knew the game of basketball very well. He knew how to motivate Michael Jordan to use his natural talent in order to be one of the best basketball players in history.

So why would you need a coach anyway? For some reason we seem to be more accountable to others than we are to ourselves. If I need to lose a few pounds, I tend to cheat less if I'm dieting with a friend than if I'm dieting on my own. A coach gives structure to your actions and holds you accountable, and a coach has you achieving your desired result as his or her own goal.

So now you might be wondering, "How do I hire the *right* coach?" You should interview a number of candidates to find the right one for you—someone you feel a great vibe with and who you feel is connected to the vision you have for yourself and for your life.

To get you started, here are five questions you should ask any potential life coach:

1. What type of coaching do you specialize in?

2. Do you have any testimonials from previous clients?

3. Who are your mentors for being a coach?

4. Do you follow a certain codes of ethics?

5. Will your services be part of one-on-one or group coaching?

The common denominator with all good life coaches is that the right person is someone you will be able to count on to champion what's important to you even when you may not be able to do so yourself.

The Differences Between a Life Coach and Therapist

Coaching is often confused with therapy, so let's look at some of the differences between the two. Now, these differences have been thoroughly examined and explained by PhDs, so it's not my intent to make distinctions at that particular level. I'm just going to highlight some general differences between the two options.

Therapy is the diagnosis and treatment of psychological issues. Basically, what that means is that people usually go to therapy to begin the process of identifying, deprogramming, and reversing the mental and emotional effects of traumatic experiences. In therapy, you examine your past in order to make sense of the actions you're taking in the present. You also examine your emotions and how they are a driving force behind your actions. Different types of therapy include:

- Behavior Therapy

- Cognitive Therapy

- Dialectical Behavior Therapy

- Interpersonal Therapy

- Psychodynamic Therapy

- Family Therapy

- Group Therapy

The list goes on and there are many additional kinds of therapy, but I'm sure you get the point. In each one of the above types of therapy, can you see where there might be some mental or psychological disorders that would be addressed?

Many of these types of therapies can overlap one another. For example, if an athlete was in a car accident and she was badly physically injured and could no longer play her sport, could easily be altered, making behavioral therapy necessary.

Therapy usually begins with the therapist digging deeply into a patient's past. He or she may focus on the patient's childhood, education, cultural environment, religious beliefs, and relationship with their parents and siblings. This will help the therapist determine the root cause of the patient's current issues. The therapist may take smaller pieces of the patient's experiences over a period of time and piece them together in order to help them process the traumatic experiences that brought them to where they currently are.

Terry Hite

Coaching, on the other hand, is focused on the future you want to create and the actions you will need to take in the present to make that future a reality. Coaching deals with what's happening right now!

Just like therapy, there are different types of coaching. Some of them include:

- spiritual coaching

- career coaching

- health and wellness coaching

- leadership coaching

- network marketing coaching

- transitional coaching

- sales and marketing coaching

- writing and publish book coaching

Just as therapists do, coaches start with an initial assessment of their client in order to determine their needs. There are a series of questions the coach may ask in order to draw their conclusions. The reason for this assessment is threefold:

- To determine if the coach is knowledgeable enough to help the client.

- To determine if the client is comfortable enough with the coach to proceed.

- To determine if the coach needs to refer the potential client to another coach in a different area or to a psychologist.

The following diagram visually illustrates the difference between a coach and a therapist.

Understand that a coach and a therapist do not serve the same purpose.

To ensure that you understand the significant difference between the two, I have crafted the below scenarios for you to read and then determine whether the person in question needs coaching or therapy:

Scenario #1: Katie has moved to the United States from another country and she doesn't know many people. She wants to rebuild her medical career and make new contacts in that field. Does Katie need a coach or a therapist?

Scenario #2: Douglas has returned home after doing a tour in a war overseas. He has started to experience nightmares and he is exhibiting behavior that wasn't present before he left. Does Douglas need a therapist or coach?

Scenario #3: Olivia is happily married and has two children. She has one sister, Hannah, who has fallen on hard times financially and personally. Hannah calls Olivia regularly to ask for money and to vent about her relationship. Olivia feels bad that she's doing well and that her sister isn't. Olivia's husband starts to complain about all the time Olivia is spending with Hannah rather than with her family. Olivia wants to set boundaries with Hannah but can't bring herself to do so. Does Olivia need a coach or therapist?

Scenario #4: Franklin has been married for several years. He has a beautiful wife and four lovely children, is very comfortable financially, and is well-respected in his community. For some reason, however, Franklin is not happy. He finds it difficult to find joy in his life. He feels trapped in a lifestyle that no longer suits him, and he desperately wants to find happiness. Does Franklin need a coach or a therapist?

After reading the above scenarios, how well would you say you were able to determine the type of help each person needs? Do you think you were able to identify whether the person in question needs a therapist or a coach? Let's take each scenario one at a time and then see how you did.

Scenario #1: The goal that Katie set for herself was to build her career, meet new people, and learn more about her new environments. In this scenario Katie would benefit from a coach, as there doesn't seem to be a mental or psychological issue surrounding her goal. She may consult with a career coach to help her with advancing her medical career. The career coach may also recommend certain resources that will help Katie meet people who work in her area of expertise, and the coach may also advise Katie to join certain clubs, groups, or organizations that travel around the city and explore what it has to offer.

Scenario #2: Douglas is a war veteran who is experiencing classic signs of post-traumatic stress disorder. He will be better suited seeking treatment from a licensed professional. He needs a therapist who specializes in this specific type of disorder and would likely be referred to a specialist through the US Department of Veterans Affairs.

Scenario #3: Olivia has identified exactly what it is that she would like to do regarding her sister's behavior. She has decided that, in order to maintain happiness in her own home, it would be best for her to say no to her sister's constant requests. Olivia would benefit from the services of a coach rather than a therapist, as she hasn't revealed there to be any previous issues in her relationship with her sister. In the above scenario, Olivia has identified a specific goal she wants to achieve. Through role play and other techniques that will prepare her for the conversation she needs to have with her sister, Olivia can learn from a life coach how to say no to her sister as well as how to stick to her decision.

Scenario #4: Franklin seems to have it all. Describing his circumstances is like reading most people's wish list for a perfect life. So if Franklin has a beautiful spouse, wonderful children, plenty of money, a great career, and the respect of his community but still isn't happy, he may or may not be in need of a licensed professional. Franklin's goal seems to be abstract rather than definitive; therefore, the work of a life coach *or* a therapist could help him to better understand himself. Either professional could help in uncovering the reasons why he's not happy despite his seemingly ideal lifestyle.

So how did you do? Were you able to determine whether the people in the above scenarios needed a coach or a therapist, and if so, were you able to identify why?

If after giving your own circumstances and needs careful thought and consideration you determine that you need a coach rather than a therapist, you're in great hands.

To Change or Not to Change

Briefly, I've been discussing things you can do to improve your life, and hopefully you have found them to be of great value to you. But I want to take a moment to break down my area of specialty so you will understand why you should even listen to me in the first place.

For many years, I have been heavily involved in several processes called Change Management Methodology and Lean Six Sigma. Change management is an understanding of how to make a change successfully. Whether at home, in your community, or at work, individuals move through the change process in a conventional and expected path. For example, before a large corporation implements a new computer system, it is necessary to make sure that a great implementation plan and a great back-out plan are in place. This is done by making sure that the computer system has been tested properly so that it doesn't disrupt the flow of the business.

Simply put, it is very important to make sure that a change is conducive and beneficial to the corporation before it is implemented. A good example would be a new software system. Making sure that there's a need for it, and if there is, it is tested to validate its relevancy and low risk of disruption to the current system and to gauge any impact to the customer(s).

Lean Six Sigma, on the other hand, is defined as a comprehensive and flexible system for achieving, sustaining and maximizing business success. At the heart of the Six Sigma system is what's known as the DMAIC cycle, which is broken down as follows:

- First: *Define* the problem. Reach agreement on things like the issue(s) at hand, the scope of the project, specific goals, a timeline, and the performance target for the project and then create a project charter reflecting these decisions.

- Second: *Measure* the problem. Collect reliable data and expose the underlying causes of the problem.

- Third: *Analyze* the problem. Verify the causes affecting the key input and output variables tied to the project goals.

- Fourth: *Improve* the problem. Implement what was determined to be the best way to fix the situation.

- Fifth: *Control* the problem. Continuously and consistently improve the situation so that it doesn't get worse.

As a life coach, I have used this methodology in whole or in part to help me to guide individual clients reach their goal(s). And while I have simplified the process below, it could look something like this:

Scenario: Allison is a single parent who works part-time and is also in school. She found herself overwhelmed by all the tasks she needs to get done every day so she came to me for help in sorting out how to complete them while minimizing her stress.

Following the Six Sigma process detailed above, the solution to her problem looks like this:

- *Define* the problem: Allison created a project charter that laid out her mission, objectives, time frame, and consequences for completing her tasks. In this stage of the DMAIC process she could identify areas which should be addressed. After completing a brainstorming session to identify specific problems we continued to the next step of the process.

- *Measure* the problem: Allison determined that not all of the tasks on her plate needed to be done at the same time, on the same day. I assisted her with creating a Pareto chart to help define the level of importance and urgency of each of her tasks.

- *Analyze* the problem: Allison use of the "5 Whys" is basic in asking the question at least 5 time to analyze the root cause of her problems.

Even though we realized that there is nothing magical about the 5 whys. In fact, we were able to analyze some of the problems within 3 or 4 whys.

- *Improve* the problem: Allison prioritized each task and put them into three categories: High Priority, Complete within Forty-Eight Hours, and Less Important. She decided that she would put in a process called "Poka-Yoke" or better known as "Mistake Proofing". She put into place a "to do list" that was checked every day and alarms to remind her to check for certain events during the day.

- *Control* the problem: As more tasks come up, Allison will place them in the proper categories so that she can immediately assess if they're things that need to be done right away. If too many tasks fall into the High Priority category, she might choose to take advantage of services like TaskRabbit.com, which (if available in your area) helps you find people to run your errands at little cost, or Chore.com, which keeps track of the items on your must-do list.

There's something about putting things on paper that takes them off your mind. When you can actually see all the things you have to do in black and white that has a tendency to lessen the feeling of being overwhelmed.

I'm going to share a story that I once heard a speaker tell:

> There was a man who lived in a heavily populated city. He had a job, a car, and an apartment. At one point his employer needed to make some drastic changes, and those changes wound up altering this man's life significantly. Today that man drives a different car, lives someplace else, and holds a different position at work.

That's the end of the story. More than likely one of two thoughts entered your mind. Either you visualized a man getting a promotion, upgrading his car, and moving into a nicer place, or you thought he was demoted, that he downgraded his vehicle, and that he moved into a less desirable place. Did you notice that the story never stated whether the changes at his place of business were good or bad? Which scenario did you envision? With that answer in mind, I am compelled to ask you this key question: *How do you perceive change?*

Your reaction to the above story is a good indicator of how you assess where you are and how you truly feel about changing your situation. See, many people claim they want change, but when it comes to taking action to make change happen, some cower and some prevail. The ones who prevail are truly game changers, and those are the ideal candidates for working with a life coach.

I want to leave you with something that will forever burn in my heart and in yours. The importance of the *message* I heard from another motivational teacher which resonates with me so much, that I have to share it with you in hopes that it will spark the same fire in you that's illuminating within me.

The *message* explained how we all have different plans, different beliefs about certain things, and how we can respond to these events, and the *message* then summarized that we have one thing in common with one another as these *"Six Human Needs"* were being described:

1. **Certainty:** The need to be joyfully contented, avoid being hurt, and have some level of comfort.

2. **Uncertainty**: the need for variety, drama, spontaneity, and a chance to feel alive.

3. **Significance**: the need to feel like a one-of-a-kind, extraordinary, and important person.

4. **Love and Connection**: the need to give and receive affection and support to and from others.

5. **Growth**: the need to become more and to break through stagnation. We either grow or we die.

6. **Contribution**: the need to give beyond ourselves.

The *message* further explained that these *"Six Human Needs"* are neither right nor wrong, but their focus will either create different *opportunities and different problems*, depending on where you're at in your current life. If you give emphasis to one of the *"Human Need"* more than the other in your life, it may cause problems in other areas of your life, such as denying yourself the opportunity to grow and accomplish your goals.

Five Cs: Common Practices That Stifle the Human Spirit

In this chapter I want to address what I have found to be the five most common practices that stifle the growth of the human spirit—practices I refer to as The Five Cs. What's scary about them is that we often do them without realizing how detrimental they are. The habits have been instilled in us gradually over a long period of time, and as a result it's difficult to even recognize when we're engaging in them. What's more, when someone points out what we're doing, we become angry and resist making changes because we haven't yet recognized the behavior in ourselves.

What I am about to reveal may cause you to have an "aha" moment or raise an eyebrow, or it might fall right in alignment with what you currently know to be true. Whatever your reaction, it's important to confront The Five Cs because you can't improve yourself if you don't know where you fall short.

#1: Choosing to Live by the "Someday" Syndrome

Many of us are guilty of saying things like:

- "Someday I'm going to write that book."

- "Someday I'm going to lose weight."

- "Someday I'm going to stand up for myself."

- "Someday I'm going to go back to school."

- "Someday I'm going to start a business."

Well, ladies and gentlemen, on this day I say to you:

Welcome to someday!

Someday is no longer tomorrow or next week. Someday no longer exists solely within the realm of New Year's resolutions. Someday is no longer a faint thought in the distant future. Someday is today! Now! This moment!

Whatever it is you desire to do, whatever goal you've set for yourself, the day to make it happen is today. No more dreaming about what could be. If you want to write a book, start writing. If you want to lose weight, start eating healthier today. If you want to start a business, find a mentor. If you want to go back to school, search online for courses.

#2: Choosing to Abandon Your Goals

I can't say enough about having and sticking to goals. Goals are great because they give you something to shoot for. If you don't have goals, you are blindly moving through life without any direction.

It's very easy to give up on dreams because they seem to come true for so few people. You may look at someone else and wonder, "How did they get that?" You may even be a little envious because it seems that, no matter how hard you, try you can't get ahead. I will share with you something I once heard a successful gentleman say:

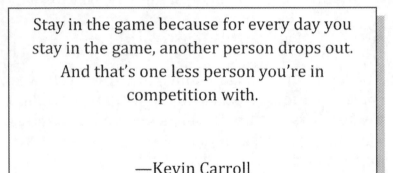

Stay in the game because for every day you stay in the game, another person drops out. And that's one less person you're in competition with.

—Kevin Carroll

When I heard that statement it resonated with me on a level that I can't explain. Don't give up. Stay the course and see your goal all the way through. How else are you going to know if you really have what it takes to succeed?

#3: Choosing to Seek Happiness from External Sources

This is a big one. This is also probably the most common of The Five Cs because from the moment we are born we look to others not just for happiness but for sustenance and knowledge. We ask our parents, teachers, friends, bosses, coaches, therapists, and other people for input about how to lead our own lives. Sometimes their advice is good and spot-on; sometimes it's not. Regardless, let me go on record as saying that happiness *does not* come from another person, a place, or an object.

There are many factors that determine how you perceive and feel yourself: your childhood experiences your parents your friends your religion your education social systems television magazines

A mistake we often make is to give people too much power over us. A good example of this is when we say things like "You make me angry" or "You make me happy." What I'm about to say to you may be an eye opener so write this on your heart:

No one can *make* you feel anything.

If I were to tell you right now to go and look in a mirror and feel sad, do you think that would happen? No, most likely it would not, because that's not how it works. Now, if I told you a sad story that might *trigger* an emotional response from you. That's certainly different from me *making* you feel sad. Do you see the difference?

The difference is that one is a trigger and the other, it would seem, requires some type of magic wand to instantly cast a spell of a specific nature upon you.

Seeking happiness from external sources will always lead to failure because the source of happiness is coming from outside of you. *Truthfully, your happiness can only come from you!*

#4: Choosing Fear over Joy

Most of us feel pretty comfortable in our own little worlds. The majority of us live in a bubble where everything may not be great but is familiar. A common habit that most people share is choosing what's comfortable and familiar over what's unnerving and unknown.

I remember reading a quote by Michael Pritchard, "Fear is that little darkroom where negatives are developed." For those of you who may not be familiar with the metaphor used here, photographs used to exclusively be developed from something called a negative in a room that was, in fact, dark. While some photographers do still work with film, most images today are digital and don't require being developed in such a way. Talk about what's not normal anymore, right?

Choosing fear over joy is especially common in personal relationships. For example, Carmen has been with Wesley for seventeen years, and overall the two of them appear to be happy—but that's from the outside looking in. In speaking with Carmen more deeply, what I discovered about her relationship was both shocking and, unfortunately, very common.

Carmen and Wesley live together in a moderately sized home in a big city. They met and fell in love at a very large church in town where Carmen is a receptionist and Wesley is a deacon. At first their relationship seemed like a dream come true. Carmen thought she had found her partner for life. Wesley was a gentleman, he complemented her, and he was kind to her friends. After about four years of being together, they got married in the church where they met and had dedicated their lives to.

Shortly after getting married, Carmen began to feel uneasy, although she couldn't quite put her finger on why. Wesley's behavior had started to change. Carmen noticed that he gave her fewer and fewer compliments, he didn't open the door for her as much, and their conversations had gone from very deep and thought-provoking to superficial. She also noticed that the frequency of their lovemaking had significantly decreased, and even when they did partake in the act it wasn't as intimate as it had been before. Whenever Carmen tried to talk to Wesley about it, he became very defensive.

Carmen began to doubt and blame herself. She thought perhaps she wasn't attractive to Wesley anymore. This sparked an incredible motivation on her part to lose weight. Although she wasn't the size she was when she and Wesley got married, she was still a very attractive woman. Because she didn't think her husband thought so, however, she was determined to change her appearance. She started by trying to lose weight the right way: she drank more water, exercised regularly, and ate healthy foods. But it seemed that the process wasn't going as quickly as she wanted it to, so she began to take appetite suppressants in order to curb her eating. When that didn't take the pounds off fast enough, she turned to more drastic measures. She started to combine multiple drugs in the hope that it would accelerate her weight loss. Ignoring the signs of illness, she proceeded to pop pills, determined to make her husband feel attracted to her again.

When the pills weren't enough, Carmen consulted a doctor about getting weight-loss surgery. The doctor explained that she wasn't large enough for her insurance to cover the procedure but Carmen didn't care. She paid for the surgery out of her own pocket and started to drastically lose weight. Carmen lost weight so quickly that she began to take on an appearance of someone who was ill. She found herself answering questions like "How are you feeling?" and "Is everything okay?" more often than she cared to. When she looked at herself in the mirror she realized that she preferred her original size to this. To make matters worse, the surgery had created a bigger wedge between Carmen and Wesley because of the financial strain that were now spreading in their relationship.

One Saturday afternoon Carmen felt that she couldn't take another day of misery in her marriage so she confronted her husband in an assertive and demanding fashion, begging him to tell her the cause of his distance. What he told her nearly knocked her off her chair. "I haven't been happy for years, Carmen," he said. "It wasn't anything you did or didn't say to me so please don't blame yourself." He went on to tell her that somewhere along the line he fell out of love with her and he couldn't quite figure out why. He also said that he didn't want to give up on the marriage and, more importantly, he didn't want to be ridiculed at their church. He stayed in the marriage to save face. Carmen admitted that she, too, had thought of leaving the marriage but was also afraid of what people at their church might say. All the years of Wesley's rejection, secrecy, and distance had shattered her self-esteem.

This scenario has two sides. First, Carmen felt that the issues in her marriage were on her shoulders alone and as a result resorted to drastic measures that were both unhealthy and financially draining. This added to her stress level and eventually she became miserable in her marriage. If Carmen had realized that who she was as a person—whether she was thin or not thin—should be enough for someone to love her, she would not have felt the need to take such drastic measures. A joyful life is being with someone who loves you just the way you are. She allowed the fear of ridicule to outweigh her joy.

The second side of this story is Wesley's side. Wesley chose to stay in a marriage that no longer served him well because of his fear of what others were going to say or think. It's possible that Wesley could have led a more joyful life if he had decided to tell his wife how he genuinely felt instead of pretending that everything was fine. In this situation Wesley also chose fear over joy.

#5: Choosing to Not Ask for Help

How unstoppable could you possibly be if you had to do everything yourself? The phrase "No man is an island" rings as true today as it did when John Donne first wrote it in the early seventeenth century. Talk to successful people and they will tell you that there is no way they could have achieved what they've achieved without the assistance of someone else.

If you want something you currently don't have, you have to do what you've never done before. If I were to tell you to go into a room and build a table, would you be able to do it? Let's assume that all the tools you need are inside the room. You have wood, nails, glue, a hammer, a level, and instructions. Would you be able to build a strong, sturdy table? If you've never done so before, the answer is likely no.

But what if you had a union carpenter in the room with you? Not only do you have all the tools you need to build your table, but you also have a professional at your side guiding you every step of the way. Would you be able to build a table then?

Every person needs help at some point in some way, whether it's in business or in life. It's important to listen to someone who has more experience than you. You have to instinctively learn to trust people—although you shouldn't automatically trust them more than you trust yourself. If you are too prideful and hardheaded, you may cause yourself to miss out on opportunities to learn.

You may be loaded with enthusiasm and confidence, but without someone to help you direct all that energy you may waste a lot of time. There is no weakness in asking for help. In fact, it's a sign of strength.

Unmasking Your True Identity

What would your reaction be if someone said to you, "I dare you to be yourself"? You may look at them confused and you may even feel a little offended, since they have seemingly assumed that you are not, in fact, being your true self. In many cases, however, they would be absolutely right. You see, there are people in this world who can decipher when a person is being genuine and when they're not. In fact, I think all of us have this capability because we all have what's called instinct, and instinct lets us know when something isn't right. Admittedly, there are some people whose instinct is much sharper than others, but most of us can generally recognize when something is awry.

In this chapter I'm going to introduce you to something called the Uncertainty Reduction Theory, which was developed in 1975 by Charles Berger and Richard Calabrese. The theory states that "people have a need to reduce uncertainty about others by gaining information about them. Information gained can then be yours to predict others' behavior."

What this means is that when you meet someone for the first time, or when you're interacting with someone you've met but don't know well, you may, consciously or subconsciously, mentally put them in certain categories in an effort to understand who they are. Once you feel confident that you've labeled them correctly, you then behave toward them in a way that corresponds with those labels.

Most of the time, our labeling a person is done without us or them ever realizing it. We are programmed to try to immediately identify a person's culture, educational level, economic status, and age bracket, etc., in an effort to help us understand who the person we're interacting with is. But consider this: While you're doing this to someone else, guess what they're doing? That's right—they're doing the same thing to you!

What that means is that two people who have just met for the first time, or two people who already know each other, try to figure out who the other is. In doing so, they are allowing their "representative" to meet the other person instead of their true self. The challenge with this is that they are communicating with each other but on a level that is only surface-deep. Nobody is genuinely getting to know anybody. In other words, they are wearing a mask.

Here I'm reminded of the movie *Eyes Wide Shut* starring Tom Cruise. There is a scene in the film where he's at a party with hundreds of people and they're all wearing masks. In some cases you can't tell if the person is male or female, which is symbolic. Think about it: How many times have you walked into a room full of people you don't know and, as a result, aren't quite sure where you fit in? Many of the other guests will smile at you, shake your hand, and perhaps even pay you a compliment, but which ones do you really click with, and which ones can you really trust? Who has your genuine interest at heart? Who is out to glean as much information about you as they can in order to deceive you in some way? A situation like that can be very scary for many people. It's no wonder that in public we often wear our own form of a mask.

There are a number of ways we try to reduce the uncertainty we feel about others:

Observing: We observe people without their knowledge in public or social settings, such as in a restaurant, at a ballgame, or on the job.

Initiating: We arrange a situation where we can encounter someone without them knowing that we set it up. For example, you inquire if someone will be at a social function and then, when the time comes, arrange to be introduced to them.

Approaching: We see someone we decide we want to meet and approach them directly, asking questions or making conversation.

Whichever of these three methods we choose, our efforts are focused on reducing our uncertainty about others when we are interacting with them and thereby eliminating as much anxiety and discomfort associated with the experience as possible.

Chances are that at some point in your life you've been hurt by someone you love or did love. You may have felt anger, surprise, devastation, and other emotions that you never want to experience again. It's because of our experience with these emotions that we build a wall around our hearts, in an attempt to protect and spare ourselves. It's no wonder, therefore, that the Uncertainty Reduction Theory is practice by nearly everyone. Nobody wants to be vulnerable to being hurt.

But no matter where you are in your life right now, whether you're happy or sad, wealthy or poor, healthy or ill, you are still a person of value. Once you understand that, you will give yourself permission to remove your mask so that people can see who you really are. Knowing they may not like you is okay, since *you* are okay with yourself.

You are the sum total of all of your experiences, good and bad, and still you are enough. You may feel less worthy than someone else or you may have been rejected by someone you love, but even if that's the case you are still enough. Who you are right now, in this moment, with all your burdens, is still a worthy human being.

> To be yourself in a world that is constantly trying to make you something else is the greatest accomplishment.
>
> —Ralph Waldo Emerson

If there's an area of your life that *you* wish to improve then do it. But let it be because it's something that you want to do *for yourself*, not for anyone else. If it's done for someone else, it won't last and it won't be fulfilling.

It's Easy to "Do You"

Just being yourself is easier said than done, but that's only because we're not always comfortable with who we really are. When you value your true self and everything that that entails, it becomes easy to "do you."

Here are some things you can do to slowly start removing your mask when interacting with people you're not yet familiar with:

Reveal something embarrassing about yourself. This doesn't have to be the most humiliating moment in your life. Instead, it could be something like the time you sent a text message to the wrong person or the time you had one too many glasses of wine at a party and danced offbeat all night long. This shows your human side, and in turn it gives the person you're talking with permission to reveal something about who they are. If you start the ball rolling it will continue to roll.

Give a genuine compliment. If there's something you enjoy about the person you're speaking with, tell them. Let them know that you like their accent, their haircut, or choice of accessories. Make sure that whatever the compliment is, however, that it's something you actually mean. Remember, everyone has instinct, and if your companion feels you're being disingenuous, you may do damage to your budding relationship.

Preface your behavior. Whenever I meet someone for the first time, I let them know that I'm really bad with names. After being introduced to them I may say something like, "I'll probably ask you three or four more times for your name before I finally remember it, so forgive me in advance and please don't be offended." Another example is that, because of my humorous nature, I may tell someone, "If you see me behaving a little goofy, don't be alarmed. That really is who I am," and then I cast a really big smile. Remember, you can't really expect other people to like you until you like yourself. Removing your mask gives other people permission to remove theirs.

Imagine the type of world or society we would have if everyone revealed who they truly are. It would eliminate gaps in communication, altercations, assaults, and even more. So for the sake of your sanity, and mine . . .

Remove the mask.

Living Your Life with a Purpose

Living your life's purpose can seem like an abstract if not impossible thing to do, especially when you didn't grown up in an environment that encouraged talking about such a thing or even acknowledged that such a thing existed.

I'm sure many of you can recall being asked by your parents or caregivers what you wanted to be when you grew up and that you responded with things like fireman, astronaut, movie star, and so on. I would venture to say, however, that very few of you growing up were asked, "What is your life's purpose?" If you *were* asked that question, you likely wouldn't have known what to say. You probably would have looked at your parents with a blank stare, indicating that you needed clarification. If you were anything like me as a child you were easily distracted, so a deep, thought-provoking question would not have received as much attention as the toys you were playing with at the time did.

The question of what one's life purpose is can be difficult for adults to answer as well. After all, many people, in spite of having lived many years, experienced many things, and visited a number of places; still stumble when it comes to answering this (not-so) simple question. I've therefore created a few categories that will help you get a head start in answering this question honestly and without hesitation, as clarifying one's life purpose is something a life coach will help you with throughout the course of your working relationship.

Focusing Your Energy

Having clarity and focus start with having clear goals in knowing what your life's work is really about. But before I continue, I want to clarify what the word *work* means in this context. When I say "work," I don't want you to think of it in terms of a job. Instead, I want you to think of it as more like a mission. Think of your goal as something that you focus your energy on and that you can see off on the horizon. Your work, or your mission, is to journey through your present circumstances and conditions to get to that goal on the horizon without stopping. Work is generally something that we think we *have* to do in order to survive, but your life purpose should not be viewed in this way. Instead, view your life purpose as your significant contribution to yourself and to the world.

Clarity and direction also come from knowing what makes you happy. Earlier in this book we looked at things that were considered the norm many years ago but today are not. Define for yourself what makes you happy rather than pursue what society says should make you happy. Not everyone wants a big house, a fancy car, a seven-figure income, and an elite social circle. In fact, many happy people I've encountered over the years don't have any of those things. They're very content with their economy car or bicycle, their small home in the country, their moderate income that sustains them, and their small circle of close friends. They've created a life that's in alignment with what genuinely makes them happy.

This isn't to say that having certain luxuries in life don't bring about a *sense* of happiness, because sometimes they do. However, usually that kind of happiness is only temporary, since true happiness doesn't come from possessing things. Happiness comes from within, and a happy person may or may not choose to live a luxurious lifestyle. Do you see the difference?

> If you don't design your own life plan, chances are you'll fall into someone else's plan. And guess what they have planned for you? Not much.
>
> Jim Rohn

Your life's purpose is woven into your day-to-day life. It is *not* an abstract, unattainable thing. But you can't define the purpose of your life without clarity and focus.

Below, enter yes or no as it pertains to the following statements in order to gauge how in touch you are with your life purpose:

_____ I have clear goals and focus.

_____ I am clear about my life work.

_____ I know what makes me happy.

_____ I feel like I'm on track in my daily living.

If you answer no to any of the above questions then a life coach can give you the advice needed to guide you onto your path of achievements.

Finding Fulfillment in the Workplace

Have you ever met someone who dreads going to work? Whenever the subject of their job comes up they do things like sigh heavily, roll their eyes, frown, or begin to tell you a story about one of the many horrible experiences they've had on the job.

People's jobs are one of the primary areas in which they don't feel they're living their life purpose. Unfortunately, since bartering is no longer practiced in a world where the original form of currency is mainstream and therefore people have to go to work to earn a living.

The work you choose to do should be in alignment with your core values, which are the values that govern your choices on a daily basis. When your line of work reflects what you genuinely believe, it feels less like work.

The work that you do should allow you to express and develop your unique talents, gifts, and abilities. As someone who has a lot of experience in managing teams, I've come to realize that a team is more productive when each person is assigned a task they genuinely enjoy doing. It's not enough that they're good at it, since that doesn't necessarily mean they enjoy it doing it. It's not enough to be efficient; there has to be enjoyment as well.

It's also important for people to feel that the work they're doing is making a positive contribution to others' lives. What good is all the work you're doing if it benefits no one?

Another crucial element is earning the income you desire. This is usually rated as employees' second most important concern, just after enjoying the kind of work they do. Although you may feel fulfillment from performing your job, not making enough money to live comfortably creates a strong shift in your overall well-being.

Below, enter yes or no as it pertains to the following statements:

_____ My deepest values are reflected in my work.

_____ I can express and develop my talents, gifts, and abilities in my work.

_____ I feel that I'm making positive contributions to others through my work.

_____ The income I earn is a desired amount for the work I do.

_____ My work environment complements my personality.

_____ I enjoy relationships of cooperation, mutual respect, and support with my coworkers.

If you answer no to any of the above questions then I suggest you seek to gain greater opportunities for happiness and fulfillment by working with a life coach.

Facing Life's Adversity

None of us is immune to facing challenges in life. In fact, challenges are what build our character. A life without challenge is a life without the pleasure of fulfillment. I've been through many challenges in my life, and while some of them I wish to never repeat, others I look back on and actually smile about because of the lessons they taught me.

Many of those lessons are ones I'm teaching in this book. Life truly is a circle. I learned from others, and what I learned from them I am passing on to you. You will likely pass them on to people you know, and so the cycle continues.

Because we are not immune to adversity, we may as well learn how to face it head-on. I challenge anyone who says that they are living a fulfilling life that is absent of challenge and adversity.

There are many people who are lucky enough to realize what their life purpose is, but due to the trials and tribulations that often accompany its pursuit, they choose to stay where they are, in a place that's familiar to them. When that happens, not only do they cheat themselves out of living a fulfilling life, but they cheat the rest of the world as well. You have something to say and the world needs to hear it! So if you are someone who has realized your life's purpose, *don't you dare* shy away from it for any reason. After all, living your life's purpose is the ultimate goal of fulfillment and to come close is landing amongst the stars.

Below, enter yes or no as it pertains to the following statements:

_____ I'm proud of the way I react to adversity.

_____ If too much time passes without any challenges I get nervous.

_____ I believe I have a message to share with the world.

_____ Living my life purpose scares me.

_____ I have a really good idea of what my life purpose is and I'm excited about it.

There are many aspects of your life that you want to consider when assessing whether or not you are living your life purpose, because sometimes it's not clear whether or not you are. So how can you tell? Examine the diagram below. On a scale from one to five, one being the lowest and five being the highest, rank how you currently feel about your life in the following areas:

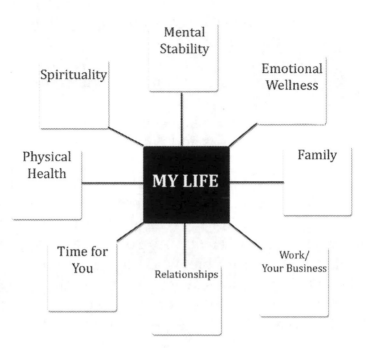

After ranking each one of these areas of your life, think about how you feel about the numbers. Do they disturb you? Are you deeply satisfied with them? Or do your feelings fall somewhere in between? Either way, you can clearly see how you view your life at this moment, which is an excellent place to start when trying to determine if you are living your life purpose.

Now we're going to do that exercise again, but this time I want you to enter the numbers as if you were living your ideal life:

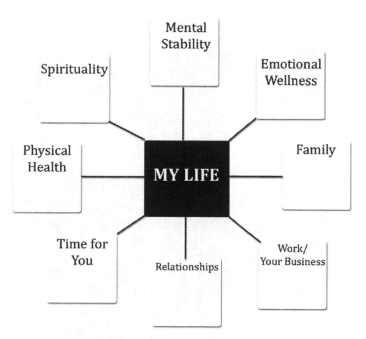

In the above chart you have entered the number in each category based on where you would like your life to be. How does this chart compare to the first chart? Are you close? Are you way off the mark? Or are you somewhere in between?

Regardless of where you fall, understand this:

Nothing ever comes to one that is worth having
except as a result of hard work.

—Booker T. Washington

Creating a Presence
Versus
Creating an Income

First, I want to define what it means to create a presence. Creating a presence refers to the undeniable energy and authority that is associated with you and your life. This energy is carried with you wherever you go, and it is felt by those you come in contact with. In many cases it can still be felt long after you've left a room.

This presence, however, can go one of two ways: It can be either positive or negative. The choice is up to you. What type of impact do you want to make on the lives of others? Do you want to be seen as a ray of light and positivity or as a plague of darkness? I think it's safe to say you would rather be a ray of light in other peoples' lives. I'm sure you would want to be someone that people look forward to being around as opposed to someone that is simply being tolerated.

Allow me to explain what is meant by creating a presence versus creating an income. For many people success has to do with the size of one's bank account, so their focus becomes making a lot of money.

However, just because you make a lot of money doesn't mean you are an inspiration to others.

In the never-ending quest to make that next dollar, somewhere along the line you lose who you really are when money remains your primary focus. I understand the importance of being able to make a living and to support yourself and your family. That is a basic need for all of us, and as a result it's very easy to fall into the trap of staying in a job you care nothing about for the sake of being able to put food on the table. Most of us have experienced this, and it feels as if you are in a miserable rut.

But I have great news—a life coach can help you assess where you are right now and help you strategize and create a plan to get you out of that rut for good. When you have someone who will champion your cause, you don't feel like you have to go it alone. When someone is present who sees your inner light—even when you can't see it yourself—there is a sense of relief because you realize that you have a partner who will help you get where you truly belong.

I once had a young client named Kevin who himself was in a rut. He was in his early twenties, worked at a local bank full-time, and was engaged to be married the following year. He graduated from college with a degree in business because that's what his parents pushed him to do. After graduation he found himself regretting the fact that he didn't pursue the major he wanted to, which was graphic design. So here he was a college graduate with a degree he didn't want or need, and a job he hated. So he hired me to help him figure out what to do.

I met with him at a café, and during our meeting his mind started to drift. I could tell he had checkout out a bit because he was no longer looking at me but doodling on a cocktail napkin instead. I regained his attention and asked him what he was thinking about. He proceeded to tell me about a dream he had the night before that contained an image he couldn't get out of his mind. I glanced down at the napkin and saw that he had made a beautiful illustration. Clearly this man was a visual person who had an amazing artistic talent.

Instantly, I was flooded with ideas on how I could help him. After we were able to assess where he currently was and where he wanted to be in the future, we created a one-year plan to get him closer to being a full-time graphic designer. It was because of his drawing that I was heavily inspired to help his dreams come into realization. Sitting in that café, I felt his genuine presence, which was that of an artist, not a banker.

I coached Kevin on how to gradually shift his focus and efforts to creating illustrations so that he could let his true presence be felt by the world. When we first met he was creating an income, and now I'm honored to say that he is creating a presence.

Achievement is not the most important thing. Authenticity is.

—Author unknown

Taking Steps to Make Real Changes In Your Life

At this stage in the process you've thought a lot about where you are in life, and you've determined that you are not only ready for change but are willing to take the actions necessary to make it happen. So, what do you do now?

➢ Now that the fire is burning.

➢ Now that you feel like getting started.

➢ Now that you want to take control of your life.

You might want to step back, take a good look at your life, and consider getting some one-on-one support from a life coach.

In order to help you figure out what your next step will be, I want to share with you a poem I wrote to keep the mind focused on the ultimate reason of why a life coach is desirable.

A Bridge for All to See

There is a bridge that extends our existence in time that expands life principles and captivates the mind.

When crossing this bridge it teaches us, "Why life?" The answers can be seen in the distance. So open up your mind to a new way of living, and do not harbor any resistance.

There is a bridge that crosses over to another way of thinking, that shows us how to leave our past behind. For when it is your turn, my friends, to cross this bridge, hopefully life's ultimate treasures you will find.

This bridge was built from the toils of the mind, life's lessons giving and forgiven at every turn. It reaches into your inner soul to span and restore the needed bridges you burned.

You have to take one step, one day, one moment at a time to get to the other side. Yet once you choose to start you'll begin to run, and life by the grace of God will be your teacher and guide.

This bridge was built from many lessons learned, and oh how happy we all would be. If only we can help, and guide one person to a bridge for all to see.

And remember . . .

When you want to do something, you don't drag your feet on it.

When you seek out help to achieve your goal, get a coach to make it clear.

When you need to accomplish a goal, you don't have to reinvent the wheel!

Goal Setting?

Here are some questions which could help you to think about some goals that you would like to set. You do not need to answer all the questions and there may be a question that's not listed here. All in all, these are some great questions which could help you get started on achieving your goal!

> Who would you like to become personally or professionally?

> What would you like to create?

> What are your career goals?

> Where would you like to go, do, or be?

> What would you want to learn?

> How do you want to feel about yourself?

> What are some fears you want to conquer?

> Who would you like to meet personally?

> Would you like to dance or learn to sing?

> What are some of your spiritual goals?

> What books would you like to read?

> Would you like to act or speak in public?

➢ Would you like to write a book?

➢ Would you like to become a big brother/big sister?

➢ Would you like to learn to be on time?

➢ Would you like to learn time management?

➢ What weight do you want to be?

Terry Hite

As you think about the questions on the previous page, write your answer here. Don't waste time thinking about your goal for now. You want to treat this like a brain storming exercise and write your goals down as quickly as possible.

❖ _____

❖ _____

❖ _____

❖ _____

❖ _____

❖ _____

❖ _____

❖ _____

❖ _____

❖ _____

❖ _____

❖ _____

❖ _____

❖ _____

Now, this is where you want to stop and think about the goals that you wrote down on the previous page. From your list of goals, select your top four goals, and briefly explain why you want these to be your top goals to achieve. It is very important after you write your goals down that you do something immediately to start to work on them. For example, if one of your four goals is to become a public speaker, then contact "Toastmaster Club" to see what it is that you need to do to get started. Please do not write down a goal and do nothing!

1. _____
   _____
   _____
   _____

2. _____
   _____
   _____
   _____

3. _____
   _____
   _____
   _____

4. _____
   _____
   _____
   _____

Now be good to yourself and go get a coach!

When I stand before God at the end of my life, I would hope that I would not have a single bit of talent left and could say, "I used everything you gave me."

—Erma Bombeck

Never be bullied into silence. Never allow yourself to be made a victim. Accept no one's definition of your life; define yourself.

—Harvey Fierstein

If you're trying to achieve, there will be roadblocks. I've had them; everybody has had them. But obstacles don't have to stop you. If you run into a wall, don't turn around and give up. Figure out how to climb it, go through it, or work around it.

—Michael Jordan

Notes

Notes

Notes

Notes

Notes

Notes

Notes

Notes

Notes

Notes